S.H.E
She Has Evolved

Journal

Juanita Walters

DEDICATION

TO EVERY GROWING PRINCESS AND EVERY
RISING QUEEN, I DEDICATE THE PAGES OF
THIS JOURNAL TO YOU! I PRAY THAT AS
YOU EVOLVE INTO WHO GOD HAS CREATED
YOU TO BE, YOU PEN YOUR JOURNEY TO
THESE PAGES SO THAT IT BECOMES AN
INSPIRING TESTIMONY USED TO EMPOWER
WOMEN ACROSS THE GLOBE!

I AM MY SISTER'S COVERING!

I AM EVOLVING INTO GREATNESS!

I AM EMBRACING GROWTH AND CHANGE!

I NEED YOU TO KNOW THAT YOU ARE
VALUABLE AND IMPORTANT!

WITH LOVE YOUR SISTER

SHE HAS EVOLVED

Principal Rochelle Hinds, AP Yvette Padilla, AP Alexandria Frank, Mrs. Towanna Hawkins (Guidance Counselor/GEM Mentor), Ms. Juanita Walters (Teacher/GEM mentor), Janice Mclean (Admin. Intern), and our Precious Pearls GEM's **(Girl Empowerment Movement)** would like to dedicate this journal to you. This is our token of appreciation to every GEM mentor, GEM mentee, GEM leaders and facilitators! We love you and we stand in with you as a circle of support!

"Evolving together as sisters!"

"Embracing the journey, blossoming, and living out our dreams!"

ACKNOWLEDGMENTS

Thank you to Deputy Superintendent Tamra Collins, Field Support Liaison Irene Spence, and Superintendent Dr. McBryde Jr. for supporting our girls through the GEM (Girl Empowerment Movement) program. We truly appreciate your support and dedication to our girl's academic and socio-emotional growth and success. To every Principal, Assistant Principal, Teacher, Guidance Counselor, school staff, facilitator/event coordinator, parent, and all who have taken part in supporting our girls through the GEM program. Your support and dedication doesn't go unnoticed! We value and appreciate your time, resources, encouragement, and love. Thank you Mr. Beaubrun for helping create the cover. A special thanks to every young princess dedicated to the process of growing and walking in destiny. We couldn't do this without you! You are important and valued! Thank you for allowing us to be a part of your journey!

This Journal belongs to:

"Welcome to the Evolution!"

This is the process of the seed being planted, the roots being secured, and the watering it takes to cause the flower to bloom!"

S. H.E
Written by Juanita Walters

She

She Has Evolved
Meticulously meeting the ground face to face
Waiting for the transformation to take.....
Her body spins round and round until the warmth of breath
has gracefully been encased...

She

She Has Evolved.....
Seasons have turned into the chapters of her life
and now since there's light.....
Her colors spill into the depths of the sky
They marvel at her wonder.......
She looks like no other.......
Not even the former......

She

She Has Evolved
Much stronger
She can adapt and endure the distance much longer!
She Has Evolved
Through His love
She has come into the knowledge of her beauty and power

She

She Has Evolved
No longer this world can design
She...... His workmanship has been defined
From the beginning of time........SHE HAS EVOLVED!!

She Has Evolved

Along this journey I'm carrying;
Perseverance, Dedication, Heart, Faith, Hope,
Trust, and the GEM Core Values:

CONFIDENCE

STRENGTH   RESPECT

HONESTY

                    BEAUTY

INDIVIDUALITY   VOICE

She Has Evolved

S (She)
- ➢ Who is she?
- ➢ What is her background?
- ➢ Where is she planted?

H (Has)
- ➢ What was her turning point?
- ➢ What initiated her shift?
- ➢ Who's instrumental in her turning point? (Divine Connections)
- ➢ What transformation is taking place?

E (Evolved)
- ➢ How has she matured?
- ➢ What's the evidence of her change?
- ➢ What has the process produced?
- ➢ The revealing............................PURPOSE UNCOVERED!!

Girl you know that you're a precious treasure whose sparkle and shine light up a room! The confidence, strength, and respect you exude are more than enough to empower everyone to the moon!

Every step you take illuminates a path for your fellow sister. You're an inspiring trendsetter whose words paint a powerful picture of confidence, respect, and strength! You are a force to be reckoned with!

May your hopes and dreams act as paintbrushes painting a beautiful scene of endurance and prosperity! You're a GEM, a keeper at that, trust and believe the power within won't let you slack! Plus your sisterhood has your back!

By Juanita Walters

She Has Evolved

_____

_____

_____

_____

_____

_____

_____

_____

_____

_____

She Has Evolved

She Has Evolved

She Has Evolved

_____

_____

_____

_____

_____

_____

_____

_____

_____

_____

_____

_____

_____

_____

_____

_____

_____

_____

_____

_____

_____

_____

_____

_____

_____

_____

_____

_____

She Has Evolved

"Mistakes can be the golden gate where transformation takes!"
by: Juanita Walters

Trust that in due season, the work started in you will come full circle! Yielding to the process will allow you to walk into your destiny!

_____

_____

_____

_____

_____

_____

_____

_____

_____

_____

_____

_____

_____

_____

_____

_____

_____

_____

_____

_____

_____

_____

_____

_____

_____

_____

_____

_____

_____

_____

_____

_____

_____

_____

_____

_____

_____

She Has Evolved

"Walk boldly, unapologetically, unashamed, unshakable, uncompromising, uninhibited as you evolve into what you were created to be!"

"Rejoice in the understanding that your process will be like no other. Although you may share similar valley and mountaintop experiences, your process is uniquely and strategically designed just for you!!"

She Has Evolved

"Understand that you're a beautiful masterpiece with intricate details that will evolve over time. Don't rush the process, don't despise the process, don't covet another's process, and don't judge another's process."

"You're on your way to a destiny/dream fulfilled!!"

I can't wait to see you Beautiful!!

Made in the USA
Middletown, DE
02 December 2022

16823075R00062